CHANGE IS INEVITABLE.

INNOVATION IS OPTIONAL.

GET CURIOUS
· *and* ·
GROW

Diana Kander

Published by True Folio.

ISBN (HC) 979-8-9923765-0-0
ISBN (eBook) 979-8-9923765-1-7

Library of Congress Cataloging-in-Publication Data
Library of Congress Control Number: 2025902014

Printed in the United States of America
19 20 21 22 23 LSC 10 9 8 7 6 5 4 3 2 1

GET CURIOUS
· *and* ·
GROW

Diana Kander

TrueFolio
PUBLISHING

Want to bring more curiosity and innovative thinking to your organization?

Here are four keynotes (drawn from this book) that Diana can deliver at your next event:

1. Unleash the Innovator Within: Diana's **signature keynote** on protecting ourselves from complacency and stagnation. This keynote is filled with laughs, insightful case studies, and easy to implement innovation strategies that attendees can use immediately, in both their personal and professional lives.

2. Innovate to Sell: Diana's sales-focused keynote designed to help sales teams prioritize what matters, eliminate distractions, and reimagine their strategies.

3. The Leader's Role in Innovation: Diana's empowering keynote on how leaders can create an environment that fosters creativity, curiosity, and continuous growth.

4. Custom Keynote: Inspired by this book? Dream up your own topic, and Diana will help make it a reality (she loves a good challenge).

For more information, please visit: www.DianaKander.com

CONTENTS

Hey there!

I'm so glad you're here! And I know how special you are.

Don't worry, you won't have to read the book in the same order as everyone else.

Please look through the options below, select the one that best describes you, and follow the instructions.

OPTION A

If someone familiar with my work handed you this book, and you have no idea who I (Diana Kander) am, please turn to page 12.

OPTION B

If you heard me speak at a conference, and you want to relive the magic and dive deeper into the ideas, please turn to page 26.

OPTION C

If you're considering hiring me for a keynote speech and you just want to understand if I'm a good fit for your event, please turn to page 28.

OPTION D

If you don't fit into A, B, or C, please flip to page 30.

OPTION A

Hello!

I hope you're here of your own free will and this isn't required reading, but either way, I've tried to keep this book short and fun.

First, just a bit about me.

I was born and raised in the Soviet Union, a country where being curious and innovative were all but illegal.

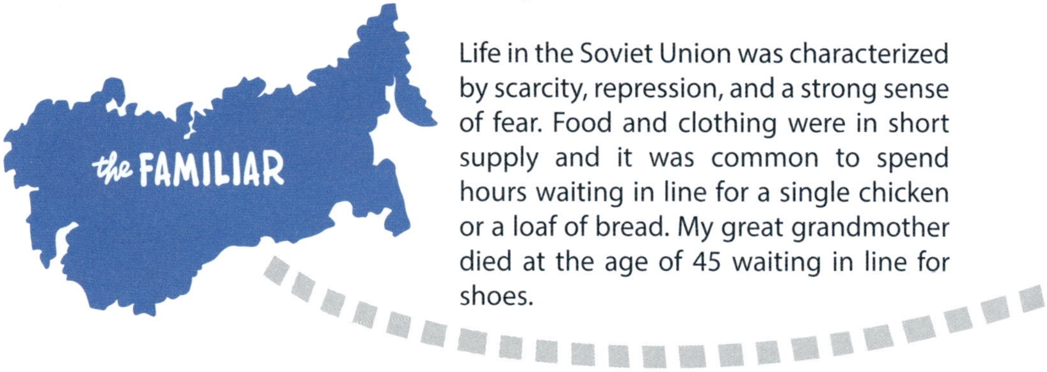

Life in the Soviet Union was characterized by scarcity, repression, and a strong sense of fear. Food and clothing were in short supply and it was common to spend hours waiting in line for a single chicken or a loaf of bread. My great grandmother died at the age of 45 waiting in line for shoes.

To make matters worse, the government controlled nearly every aspect of our lives. There was no freedom of speech and even criticizing the government in private conversations could lead to severe consequences.

Basically, it was the kind of place where no one ever smiled in photos (I have the family pictures to prove it).

In 1989, when I was 8 years old, my parents decided to flee with extremely limited resources and no real plan for where they were going. I remember my grandmother, Bella, being very opposed to the idea. Even though life was terrible, she was operating out of fear as she tried to plead her case that we should stay.

The four of us (me, my parents, and my grandmother) lived in a small apartment, in Odessa, Ukraine, so I could hear them arguing about it over many evenings.

Thankfully, my parents, just 30 years old at the time, didn't listen. They chose hope over fear and were able to bring our family, including Grandma Bella, to America.

At eight, I learned a very important lesson:

THE STATUS QUO HAS A STRONG GRAVITATIONAL PULL.

We cling to our routines and surroundings, even if they aren't serving us, because of our fear of the unknown.

But my parents taught me that we can break free from this powerful force if we just allow ourselves to believe that things can be better.

My parents were the first innovators I knew. Their decision to leave everything behind wasn't just about escaping hardship; it was about daring to create a new reality.

After arriving in the United States, I saw what was possible on the other side of change. The contrast between the repressive environment we left behind and the freedom we found in America was stark.

And I've learned that you don't need to be in the most dire of situations to create this kind of growth. Beautiful things can happen when you take a good situation and find a way to take it to the next level. Again and again.

This belief became the guiding principle of my career. I would go on to become the innovator that advocates for growth and change to improve the lives of others. I would fight the forces of the status quo because I knew what waited on the other side.

And that's what this book is about — unleashing the innovator inside of you. Whether you're leading a team, building a business, or just trying to make a positive change in your own life, remember: innovation isn't just about creating something new; it's about

DARING TO SEE BEYOND WHAT IS TO WHAT COULD BE.

So let's get started. After all, the future won't wait. And neither should you.

Do you know what Snoop Dogg is up to these days?

Have you seen his commercials for Corona, Bic, or Skechers? Perhaps you remember his numerous business partnerships with longtime pal Martha Stewart, including a TV show and a cookbook?

Not to mention his continuously successful solo albums and star-studded, genre-spanning musical collaborations. Perhaps you've even heard about his youth football program, which trains kids from the inner city in both football and interpersonal skills to prepare them for college and a variety of professions.

This abbreviated list doesn't even scratch the surface of Snoop's current exploits. He opened up some real estate in the Metaverse and sold the "properties" next door to his virtual house for a total of $1.2 million. In the Metaverse!

As part of his 2022 album release, he sold $44 million worth of NFTs. (Are those still a thing?)

He's an official Olympic commentator for NBC.

Snoop also has a children's YouTube channel called Doggyland. It features nursery rhymes and kids' songs. He has his own line of breakfast food (including Snoop Loopz cereal), his own wine label, a pet apparel business, and — of course — a cannabis company.

Ever hear of Esports? It's competitive video gaming. Well, Snoop started his own Esports league. It's called Gangsta Gaming.

Oh. And he founded a $100 million investment fund.

OK, OK. You get it. He's everywhere. Doing everything.

Now, let's contrast Snoop Dogg with another rapper who was also popular in the '90s, Vanilla Ice. Do you know what Vanilla Ice is up to? You might remember he had a TV show for a bit about house flipping.

What else? It's hard to think of anything, isn't it?

Mostly, Ice is headlining the "I Love The 90s" reunion tour alongside artists like Naughty by Nature, C+C Music Factory and Color Me Badd. Coming to a city near you!

I became aware of both Snoop Dogg and Vanilla Ice when I first came to the US. They were both talented, hardworking, smart individuals who hit it big in music around the same time. At one point, Vanilla Ice's records were actually outselling Snoop's.

But today, one of them is more relevant to every age group and region in the world than he was 30 years ago. Meanwhile, the other is like, "Hey, remember 30 years ago? That was awesome!"

What this demonstrates is that we can be talented, successful, and hardworking, and still not evolve with our changing surroundings. That's because **change is inevitable, but innovation is optional.**

A quick note about the word "innovation." I'm not talking about inventing a flying car or a new type of shoe material (although if one of those is on your list of goals, the advice in this book should help you get there, too). To me, innovation means leveling up how we do our work. It's about continuous growth and adapting to our fast-changing surroundings, without letting ourselves get too comfortable.

And I'm constantly asking myself, "Self, how innovative am I being, on a scale of Vanilla Ice to Snoop Dogg?"

CHANGE

is

INEVITABLE

but

INNOVATION

is

OPTIONAL

Maybe you can reflect on the same question. On a scale of 1–5, if Vanilla Ice = 1 and Snoop = 5, how much are you innovating at work?

This is a book about how to increase that level of innovation.

Why bother? Because the world is evolving faster than ever before, and in order to keep up, we need new tools, practices, and beliefs to find a better way even when we've got something that works.

You can stop, collaborate, and listen for only so long. At some point, you have to move on to the next episode.

OK, I know that's a Dr. Dre lyric, but Snoop raps on that track, too.

So...

what do you think slows down innovation in your organization?

I'll share some common answers on the next page, but I'd love for you to take a second to **write a short list of your own**.

(No peeking at the next page.)

Does your list include:

- **Bureaucracy and red tape?**
- **Risk aversion?**
- **Lack of resources?**
- **Resistance to change?**
- **Silos and lack of collaboration?**
- **A short-term focus?**
- **Insufficient leadership support?**

Those are good, but here's the big obstacle I guarantee you didn't have on your list: **Your success.**

It might feel odd to list your success as an obstacle, but I believe it's the single greatest hindrance to growth and innovation.

Whether it's in our work, our hobbies, or our daily tasks, once we've figured out what works and we feel good about what we're doing, we hit a Success Plateau. And we get comfortable. Our rate of learning and improving drops dramatically and the influx of new insights and ideas slows way down.

This Success Plateau is where curiosity dims and innovation falters.

It's understandable! It's human nature to enjoy the view from the top, to rest on our laurels. That is the strong gravitational pull of the status quo.

But what if I told you that beyond this Plateau lies uncharted territory, ripe for discovery and primed for the kind of innovative thinking that propels careers and companies forward?

Let's look at it from a different perspective.

Think of a household task at which you consider yourself an expert. For example, I'm an expert at loading the dishwasher, in stark contrast to my husband, whose method is, dare I say, haphazard. After 25 years together, it's still stunning to me how he loads it differently each and every night. Never the correct way.

What's your expertise at home? Laundry? Vacuuming? Lawn mowing?

Seriously. Have in your mind a household task at which you are an expert.

Now ask yourself, do you read articles on how to do that task better? Do you search YouTube for videos on how to enhance your skills?

Of course you don't! You're an expert! It would be a huge waste of time to read those articles or watch those videos. What could you possibly learn?

Now, when it comes to facing down a household task you're not so sure about — whether it's cleaning the oven, repotting a plant, or braiding a kid's tangled hair — you're much more likely to turn to the internet for guidance. But your expert tasks? Not a chance. Because you've got this, right?

Don't get me wrong. That expertise is a strength. Of course it's good to be an expert. But it's also what holds us back, because we experts believe that we already know what we need to know about the topic.

Is there an even better way to do that household task that you've already mastered?

There's always a better way to do it. But our expertise extinguishes our curiosity to learn more.

Curiosity is the space between what we know and what we want to know.

And when we're an expert, there's no space there. As experts, we don't have time for curiosity; we have to-do lists. And that lack of curiosity, and lack of time for it, can result in missing big opportunities to improve.

That's where this book comes in. It's a toolkit for avoiding the Success Plateau and unlocking the full potential of our creativity, innovation, and growth.

Picture yourself not just as an expert but as an innovator, constantly evolving and embracing new opportunities for both personal and professional renaissance.

And this book outlines 10 essential innovation habits to help you stay at the leading edge of your work:

1. **THE 1-10 FILTER: How to make better decisions about where to invest your time**
2. **KILL THE ZOMBIES: How to prevent distractions from taking over your work**
3. **THE BLANK SHEET METHOD: How to reimagine what's possible**
4. **THE TRIPLE ZOOM: How to make sure you're solving the right problem**
5. **THE TOP 10 LIST: How to uncover your most innovative ideas**
6. **THE BETA TEST: How to use small bets to drive big innovation**
7. **ITERATE TO GREAT: How to refine your way to a win**
8. **NEVER GOAL ALONE: How to achieve any goal in record time**
9. **LEARN FROM THE WINS: How to increase your rate of improvement**
10. **FAIL FORWARD: How to use setbacks as stepping stones to success**

I can't overstate the importance of implementing these habits into your everyday work. In a constantly evolving world, staying static means falling behind.

Innovation is about challenging the status quo, no matter how well things are going. It's about seeing possibilities where others see a finish line.

Put these 10 habits to work and I'm confident you'll be well on your way to Snoop Dogg levels of growth.

And if there's a little expert inside your brain right now saying:

Please ask that inner expert to be patient and a bit more open-minded. Let's create some space and see if we might surprise ourselves with one or two helpful nuggets.

Or maybe you just want to keep reading to see if I have any more interesting Snoop facts to share (of course I do).

Whatever your reason to keep going, please turn to page 32 to continue your adventure.

Oh and as you read, if you want to ask any questions or share your thoughts about the content, feel free to send me a text message: (816) 399-0084. And as soon as I find my phone in whatever fort my kids have created to hide it, I'll respond.

OPTION B

Look at you! You're making space for curiosity!

I'm so excited that you want to dive deeper.

If you've heard me speak on this topic, this book is a powerful refresher on the concepts. Plus, there are so many additional innovation habits that you can use to supercharge your growth. And some cool posters you can print!

As you read, if you want to ask any questions or share your thoughts about the book, feel free to send me a text message: (816) 399-0084. And I'll respond as soon as my kids stop watching "Bluey" and give me back access to my own cell phone.

And if you want to go straight to the content, please go to page 32 to continue your adventure.

OPTION C

Imagine me slow clapping in celebration of you!

Bravo!

By flipping to this page you have shown both intellectual curiosity for my message and dedication to finding the absolute right keynote speaker for your event.

And if I may — and I'm just taking a wild stab in the dark — you strike me as someone with an exceptional sense of humor.

OK, OK.

I'm not going to grovel. I'm a professional.

In all seriousness, I'm grateful that you're here.

To find out a bit more about my story and why I'm so passionate about this topic, please go to page 12 (same as option A).

OPTION D

Hey! How did you get this book?!? Are you sure this is legal?

You get a do-over. If this material is brand new to you, please go to page 12 (Option A). If you believe that you're already doing well at maintaining that innovative spring in your step and want to learn some new tools, go to page 26 (Option B).

SECTION I
CREATE SPACE FOR GROWTH

"In the beginner's mind there are many possibilities, but in the expert's there are few."

Shunryū Suzuki

The more we know, the less we question. And the less we question, the slower our continued growth and progress.

We'll get into lots of ways to think outside the box and ask those big questions. But first, we need some space.

Space to set aside our "go go go" mentality and think beyond the immediate and urgent.

As experts, we often get caught up in our routines and responsibilities, leaving little room for curiosity and innovation.

You know how you have your best ideas in the shower? Or on a walk outside? Those moments of space allow your mind to wander and make new connections, helping you rise above the Success Plateau.

The good news is that we don't have to resort to taking four showers a day to give ourselves that kind of freedom to think.

The next three chapters offer three innovation habits to help you do less, better; and go from being busy to creating more value.

Habit 1

THE 1-10 FILTER

How to make better decisions about where to invest your time

"The difference between successful people and really successful people is that really successful people say no to almost everything."

Warren Buffett

When I was a sophomore in high school, I really wanted a scholarship to college. Even though my family was starting to establish our footing in America, we still had very limited resources. If I wanted to get a college degree, I would have to find a way to pay for it.

I was walking through my high school and saw a flyer for girls' basketball tryouts. I had heard of basketball scholarships to college, and I decided this would be my path forward.

However, because I grew up poor, I had never played organized sports of any kind. I had never even run a mile. In fact, the only thing I knew about fitness and nutrition came from a milk commercial that seemed to run on a loop in the late '90s. There were several different versions, but they all evangelized the magical powers of milk to turn regular people into peak physical specimens. And they all ended with an unforgettable slogan:

So, naturally, my entire approach to trying out for basketball was to drink as much milk as possible.

The first thing they had us do at tryouts was run in a big loop. I don't know what the second thing was, or anything beyond, because having spent two days drinking nothing but milk, I began foaming at the mouth during that first drill. I spent the rest of the tryout in the nurse's office.

I did not make the basketball team.

It's an embarrassing story, but what if I told you that treating dairy as a performance-enhancing drug wasn't even the worst decision I made during that ordeal?

It was deciding whether to try out for basketball in the first place.

When I saw that flyer for basketball tryouts, I asked myself,

The answer is easy.

But what if instead I asked:

As it happens, I've told this story during speaking engagements, and when I ask audiences whether I should have tried out for basketball as a way to pay for college, the overwhelming response is yes. Worth a shot, right? But when I ask them to rate the idea on a scale of 1–10, taking into account my skills and resources, it's widely agreed to be a 1 or 2.

In other words, thinking about the idea on a scale of 1–10 takes the choice from a yes to an obvious no.

Would you agree?

What we are doing here is creating a higher standard for what gets a yes. When you ask that simple yes-or-no, you will end up saying yes to a lot of 1s, 2s, and 3s.

Innovators set a higher standard. They say, I'm not going to say yes to anything below a 7 (or a number of your choosing) and instead, I'm going to save my time for better ideas.

It's easier than ever to be busy. We fill our schedules with tasks, meetings, and projects, often leading to a state of constant activity. We take on these projects until we reach 100% capacity — or, let's be honest, more like 120% — and only then do we begin to say no.

Experts are particularly susceptible to this. Driven by our commitment to excellence and the pressure to maintain a good reputation, we take on excessive responsibilities and only acknowledge the need to say "no" once we're already overwhelmed.

We evaluate each opportunity only looking for big red flags: "Do I have time for this?" or "Is this a totally bad idea?" In doing so, we end up filling our time with a lot of less-than-valuable to-dos. We're basically asking ourselves, "Is this a definite no?" and everything else becomes a Yes.

When we apply the 1-10 filter to our decision-making process, we start to differentiate between what is urgent and what is important. We learn to recognize that not all tasks or opportunities are created equal; some are pivotal in propelling us toward our goals, while others are mere distractions disguised as progress. And we significantly reduce the number of misunderstandings on our teams.

A man named Dave came up to me after a speech recently and said, "my wife and I just started using the 1-10 filter to decide where to go on vacation."

"Tell me more!" I replied.

He said that they had been climbing a mountain for two days. And it was just an awful experience. By the second day he was getting more and more upset with every hour that passed. When they finally got to the mountain top, he just couldn't hold it back. "I hope you're happy!" He snarled. "This is awful."

His wife looked at him in disbelief. "I didn't want to be here! I came here for you!"

And that's what happens when we passively say to our loved ones or our teams, "Do you want to go climb this mountain?" as a genuine question, and they hear, "I really want to climb this mountain!!"

Asking our teams how they would rate climbing a mountain on a scale of 1-10 allows us to have richer conversations. Discussing why I think your idea is a 2 and you think it's an 8 can help us uncover a lot of unstated assumptions that we've kept to ourselves. Compare that to the often tense and unproductive debate that can ensue when one person thinks it's a yes and the other thinks it's a no.

I have worked with banks that changed their loan approval process from a binary yes/no to a 1–10, leaders who stopped evaluating new projects as "good" or "not good enough" in favor of a 1–10, and marketing teams that started assessing the effectiveness of their campaigns on a 1–10 scale instead of deeming them "successful" or "unsuccessful."

In each of these cases, grading situations on a scale of 1–10 significantly increased the impact of their decisions.

Life isn't simply black and white, and asking where new opportunities fit on a 1–10 scale provides a spectrum for a more thorough assessment that better reflects the complexities of our work.

Here's a fun Snoop Dogg story. When Snoop's business manager was asked in an interview for the secret to Snoop's business success, he revealed that Snoop says no to more deals than he says yes to. And we're not just talking about bad offers here. Snoop once turned down a $2 million opportunity to DJ for a Michael Jordan party.

Whaat???

The only way you could say no to an opportunity like that is by using something like a 1–10 scale to help you decide.

Snoop shared that even though he was a big fan of Michael Jordan, he just had too many high priority projects keeping him busy at that time. It's fair to assume all those projects were 8s, 9s, and 10s. Maybe as incredible as a Michael Jordan party might be, the payoff and future dividends of Snoop's potential time investment in the event

set it at more like a 6.

(For what it's worth, DJing for a Michael Jordan party is a 10 on my scale. I don't even need the $2 million.)

The most successful individuals and organizations understand that time is a finite resource, and that **every *yes* to an idea means *no* to many others.**

Use the powerful 1–10 filter and reserve your time for opportunities that truly align with your goals. We don't have to be busy to create value. We just need to focus on the highest-value uses of our time.

My goal is for you to hear a loud buzzer in your head every time you hear a yes or no question about an investment of your time or resources. I want you to hear me in your mind saying, "Rate it on a scale of 1–10!"

By using the 1–10 filter, you'll ensure that your choices are intentional and aligned with your true priorities.

Reflection Questions:

1. Can you think of a time when you said yes to a time-consuming 1 or 2 that you could have avoided with a 1–10 filter?

2. What parts of your life or work could benefit from a 1–10 filter?

EVERY YES TO AN IDEA
MEANS NO TO MANY OTHERS.

Habit 2

KILL THE ZOMBIES

How to prevent distractions from taking over your work

"Get rid of clutter and you may just find that it was blocking the door you've been looking for."

Katrina Mayer

No matter how finely-tuned our 1–10 filter might be, how diligent we are in our decision making at the beginning of a project, distractions can still slip through the cracks, and sometimes an opportunity that seemed like an 8 or 9 can turn into a waste of time. Maybe we were wrong in our initial assessment or maybe the world has changed since our decision. No matter how pure our intentions or how great our effort,

SOME ACTIVITIES AREN'T WORTH THE TIME AND EFFORT THEY REQUIRE.

Yet chances are good we stick with them anyway, often because of a behavior pattern known as **Escalation of Commitment**: It's the idea that when something isn't quite working as expected, we double down on our commitment because we're already emotionally invested. We've already put this much time and effort in, so we push ahead even though – given the opportunity to choose today – there's no way we would opt to do this project.

In my view, this is the greatest source of waste in corporate America: these initiatives, ideas, or tasks that were once full of life and promise but just didn't turn into what we were hoping they would become.

If you think about everything you spend your time on at work, it can be plotted somewhere on a graph like this.

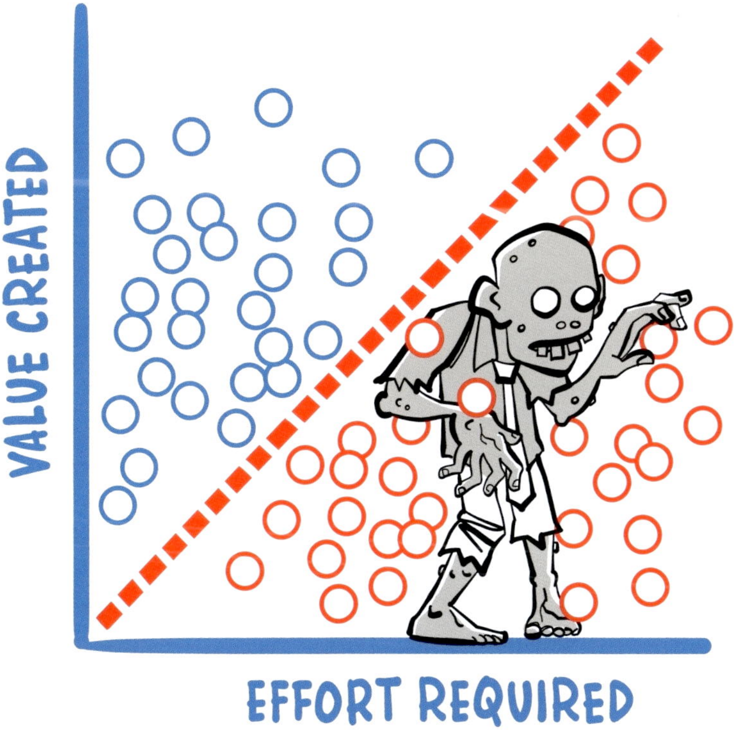

Each of the red dots signifies something that takes more time and effort to deliver than the value it's creating.

These are **ZOMBIES**, the walking dead of projects. To create space for growth, creativity, curiosity, and innovative thinking, we not only have to be diligent about our 1–10 filter; we must regularly clear out the zombies.

Zombies are outdated practices, redundant tasks, or lackluster initiatives that consume our resources without adding real value. And they are sucking the life out of our organizations!

Hunting these zombies ensures that we aren't weighed down by non–value-adding distractions. It's about

STREAMLINING OUR FOCUS.

Now, I'm not pointing fingers, but let's be real, we're all guilty of keeping these zombies around. We get comfy in our expert perches, and it's hard to admit when our brilliant ideas have turned into the office equivalent of last year's bell-bottom pants.

Especially when we're "checking in" via ego-based questions which make it nearly impossible to see things clearly. Questions like, "Did I make a bad decision?" (the answer we give ourselves is almost always no) or "Does this still have a chance of working?" (the answer we give ourselves is almost always yes).

We've built our careers on being the heroes, making the right calls, and saving the day one deck at a time. So, when it comes to admitting that some of our award-winning (in our minds) work is now just a drain on our P&L, well, that's tougher to swallow than a hand-chopped kale smoothie.

Our best bet in identifying these ideas, projects, and tasks that are impeding progress is to create a safe space to look for them.

Here are examples of the types of zombies that might be lurking in your organization:

PROJECTS

- Projects that aren't meeting expectations
- Projects that your team has no enthusiasm for
- Projects that you wouldn't invest in today if you had the opportunity to start over

RULES

- No one can explain why a particular rule exists
- The original person or reason for a rule is no longer there or it no longer makes sense

PROCESSES

- Too many layers of approval for a specific type of project
- Duplicative efforts
- Reports that aren't used
- Too many meetings, some of which are probably unnecessary
- Meetings with more than five people
- Unnecessary decks which take time to build and complicate meeting discussions
- Meetings that make people late for other meetings or don't leave time for reflection
- A process that doesn't solve the problem it was created to solve

"WHAT YOU DON'T DO DETERMINES WHAT YOU CAN DO."

-Tim Ferris

Zombies limit the amount of impact we can create. They are the reason we put in our best effort at work and don't quite feel like we're making forward progress. If we want to keep zombies from slowing down our organizations, we have to hunt and kill them on a regular basis.

Here's an example:

Vancouver City Savings Credit Union (Vancity) is Canada's largest credit union, with more than 2,600 employees and $23 billion under management.

In 2014, they launched a huge zombie-hunting project and hired a director to lead it.

The credit union was created in 1946, so you know some zombies had built up over time.

Here are their results from just their first year of zombie-hunting:

- They reviewed 430 policies and procedures, removed 152, and simplified 168 others.

- They also reviewed 310 forms, removed 79, and simplified 57.

The elimination of these zombies was huge for Vancity. It meant that they could now serve members better. For example, after the zombie-hunting effort, the process for signing up a customer went from 20 minutes to 4.

In their annual report, Vancity stated: "We believe that this work will free up our capacity for growth."

I interviewed Seema Dhanoa, the director of this program, and she told me that more than anything, the work created energy inside Vancity. "Those things that you cannot see," she said, "they are weighing down your people. They are weighing down your potential. She added:

"IF YOU WANT INNOVATION, YOU HAVE TO MAKE SPACE FOR IT."

What if you could identify initiatives that no longer do anything other than hide in your organization's P&L?

What would happen if you followed the example set by one of my consulting clients and eliminated 10,000 zombie hours of unnecessary work? (I'd love to tell you more about this, but they made me sign all kinds of NDAs so that their zombies stayed between me and them.)

How much future revenue could you generate if you were able to shift resources away from zombie initiatives and focus on new growth opportunities instead?

This applies in our personal lives as much as it does in our professional lives. Sometimes we just overcommit ourselves to too many things and end up doing all of them poorly.

Take it from the ever-wise sage Matthew McConaughey.

In the '90s, he found himself overcommitted: There was his music label, his production company, business investments, a charity, family commitments, and of course, his career as an actor.

These projects all may have all passed his 1–10 filter when he initially agreed to them, but over time at least a few of them had turned into zombies — which were draining him of the energy and creativity to excel at the initiatives really worth his time.

"I was making C pluses in everything," he said. "And when I got rid of five [commitments] and concentrated on the three I really wanted, I started making As."

Or, as Jim Rohn said:

DON'T MAJOR IN

We can all be more effective if we do **less, better**.

So, what's the game plan?

We've all got those projects that have minimal signs of life. Initiatives that sounded good in the quarterly report but are just masquerading as progress.

Let's roll up our sleeves and go full Marie Kondo on our task list, clearing out the clutter and making room for what actually "sparks joy" — or, you know, profit. Let's follow the lead of Vancity Credit Union and hunt those zombies like we're competing for a minimalist award. More than just tidying up; this will spark significant growth in productivity and morale.

If you'd like to go zombie-hunting with your team, I've put together a helpful facilitation guide. You can download it at www.DianaKander.com/Better.

Reflection Questions:

1. Can you think of some potential zombies that might be affecting your work?

2. What is the easiest one to eliminate?

Habit 3

THE BLANK SHEET METHOD

How to reimagine what's possible

"If you can dream it, you can do it."

Walt Disney

Every dollar we make is a reason not to change anything. And some of us are blessed with a lot of reasons to resist change.

The problem is that this comfort with what works can turn our strengths into weaknesses if we don't continue to grow with our quickly evolving surroundings. This is the difference between expert thinking and innovative thinking.

I once interviewed electrical engineer

STEVE SASSON,

the man who invented the hand-held digital camera in 1975 while working at Kodak. He began his pitch to senior leaders this way: "I present to you the first filmless camera!"

When Steve finished his presentation, the executives decided to hide his invention and never mention it to the outside world. At the time, Kodak made 90% of their profits from selling film. They kept Steve's invention under wraps for the next 30 years while companies all around them introduced digital cameras and took away market share.

At the time, Kodak represented the world's greatest concentration of photography expertise – expertise that duped them into mistaking a growth opportunity for a threat to their business model.

And I'll never forget what Steve told me about the pitfalls of expertise. He said, "Experts know the limitations of what's currently possible."

Expertise creates a box all around us, and then we become trapped in that box, unable to see new and better ways of working.

When we're an expert,

WE SHUT OURSELVES OFF TO WHAT IS POSSIBLE

because we've already found what works well. That's why so much innovation tends to come from outside our organization or industry. Why, for example, the horse and buggy industry didn't invent the car.

What if there was a way to avoid these constraints of "how it's always been done," or even, "how we do it today"?

This is the essence of reimagining our work — it's not an update; it's a revolution. And as experts, if we don't find a way to disrupt what we're currently doing and do it better, someone else will.

To tap into this type of breakthrough thinking, we start with a **blank sheet of paper** and ask, "How could we reimagine ________ ?"

On your team, that blank could be filled with:

- Products and services
- Sales processes
- Marketing approaches
- Meeting culture and cadence
- Employee onboarding and training
- Performance reviews
- Customer feedback loops
- Recruitment strategies

There is power in starting with a blank sheet. We aren't wed to incremental improvements on what's already working. We allow ourselves, and perhaps the newest members of our team (with their valuably fresh perspectives), to dream about how we would do something if we started from scratch.

In 2009, I found myself sitting across the table from Bo Fishback, then-vice president of entrepreneurship at the Kauffman Foundation, trying to convince him to let my startup, KR Legal Management, into a new mentorship program.

I really thought I was dropping some impressive numbers on him when I bragged about the $77,000 in revenue we generated in our first year and our plan of growing to $100,000 in revenue next year.

Across the table, Bo looked extremely unimpressed. He sat back in his chair thinking for a moment and then finally said, "I don't really care about $100,000." He paused. "I'll let you into the program if you can do $1 million in revenue next year."

I don't think his statement completely registered with me at the time. But, expressing as much false bravado as I could muster, I agreed — as if it were no big deal — to change my goal to $1 million in revenue next year. "OK, you're in," Bo said.

I walked out of the meeting thrilled to have been accepted into the program, but that feeling of elation quickly gave way to dread. *What have I gotten myself into?* I thought.

I didn't even leave the building. I found an empty cubicle not far from Bo's office, pulled out a blank piece of paper, and started adding up the numbers. At 110% capacity, doing everything I had done the previous year to the max, I could probably generate $150,000…maybe.

So I flipped the piece of paper over, wrote $1 million at the top, and started breaking down what kinds of customers I would need and what kinds of services I would have to provide to hit $1 million.

I knew I would never reach the goal doing what I was doing before. No matter how bad I wanted it or how hard I tried.

It seemed crazy, but I decided this new game plan was worth a try. The next year, my second year in business, I didn't hit $1 million, but I did generate $870,000 in revenue. That's over 1,000% growth in one year! All because I allowed myself the freedom to think about disrupting my own business rather than being stuck in incremental improvements to what was already working.

The Blank Sheet Method symbolizes endless possibilities, unburdened by current constraints. It offers freedom: the freedom to dream, to innovate, and to redefine without being weighed down by existing realities or past failures. This approach allows us to bypass incremental changes and shoot for transformative outcomes.

To reimagine is to **challenge the status quo** and

ENVISION A FUTURE UNBOUND BY THE LIMITATIONS OF TODAY.

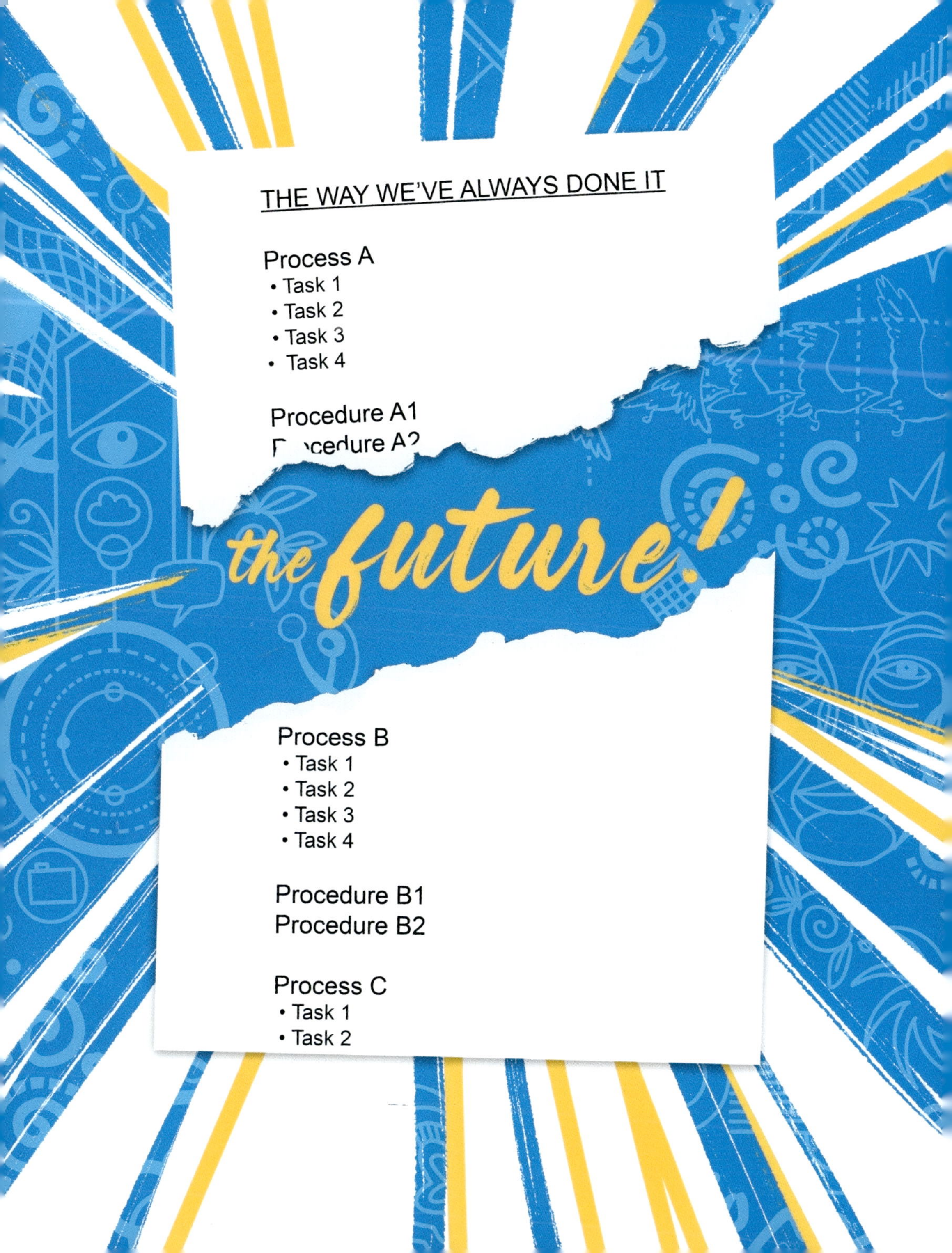

THE WAY WE'VE ALWAYS DONE IT
Process A
• Task 1
• Task 2
• Task 3
• Task 4
Procedure A1
the future!
Process B
• Task 1
• Task 2
• Task 3
• Task 4
Procedure B1
Procedure B2
Process C
• Task 1
• Task 2

Just as we reimagine processes and systems, it's crucial to turn the lens of big, Blank Sheet thinking on ourselves. What does the next version of yourself look like? Maybe it's a version where you communicate more effectively, where you prioritize mental well-being, or where you actively seek new skills.

I like to joke that my goal is to grow 20% a year so that every five years, I'm unrecognizable. I know the math on that doesn't quite work, but you get the idea.

This encourages us to continuously redefine success. Instead of measuring our worth by traditional metrics (job titles or material possessions), we seek fulfillment in the alignment of our actions with our values, and in the positive impact we have on the people in our lives. It's a shift from simply surviving to fully thriving.

In my Curiosity workshops, I often have people write a letter to themselves dated one year from our time together. And I encourage them to offer their future selves kudos and congratulations for what they have been able to achieve.

This kind of blank slate is powerful. Sometimes people surprise themselves by discovering what they really want. Sometimes they feel inspired by what's possible. But more than anything, they get clear on what reinvention could look like, and realize it's much closer than they thought.

Reflection Questions:

1. *Which parts of your work would it be powerful to reimagine?*

2. *What's one skill you want the next version of yourself to develop?*

SECTION II
REDUCE THE RISK OF NEW IDEAS

"It is not because things are difficult that we do not dare; it is because we do not dare that things are difficult."

Seneca

My specialty as an innovation consultant is working with organizations that are more than 75 years old. They wouldn't be where they are today without a lot of success behind them. And yet, what they know often gets in the way of what could be.

Every organization wants to grow and innovate, but many are worried about adding risk.

They say things like:

"Failure is not an option here. Our work is just too important."

"We cannot do anything that tarnishes our brand."

"There are tens of thousands of employees counting on us to make responsible decisions."

This cautious approach is reasonable and warranted, but it can also prevent us from trying anything new.

We need to find the balance between protecting what we have and creating the future.

So what if we could bring in some big new ideas while simultaneously reducing the risk of wasting resources or embarrassing ourselves?

We can navigate big ideas with confidence when we are guided by four established innovation habits, which we'll learn about in the next four chapters:

- **THE TRIPLE ZOOM**
- **THE TOP 10 LIST**
- **THE BETA TEST**
- **ITERATE TO GREAT**

Innovation isn't just for the fearless; it's for anyone willing to follow key principles that safeguard against the most common pitfalls.

Think of these four innovation habits as the safety net to your new aerial undertaking. You can feel confident about taking the leap when you reduce the risk of what could go wrong.

Habit 4

THE TRIPLE ZOOM

How to make sure you're solving the right problem

"It's better to solve the right problem approximately than to solve the wrong problem exactly."

John Tukey

Most of us are familiar with the classic jigsaw puzzle.

In fact, nearly 48% of Americans like to work on a jigsaw puzzle at least once per year.

It's a straightforward challenge with a simple formula: Start with the corners, create the edges, then chunk out similar color combinations, and find the right piece that fits into each empty slot to complete the picture.

This linear approach to problem-solving mirrors how we tackle issues in life:

But the truth is, the puzzles that life presents us — whether at work, in relationships, or beyond — are rarely as straightforward as jigsaw puzzles. These puzzles come in various forms, from logic puzzles to word puzzles, number puzzles, and perplexing Rubik's Cubes.

And the linear, solution-focused method just doesn't work.

Want to see what I mean?

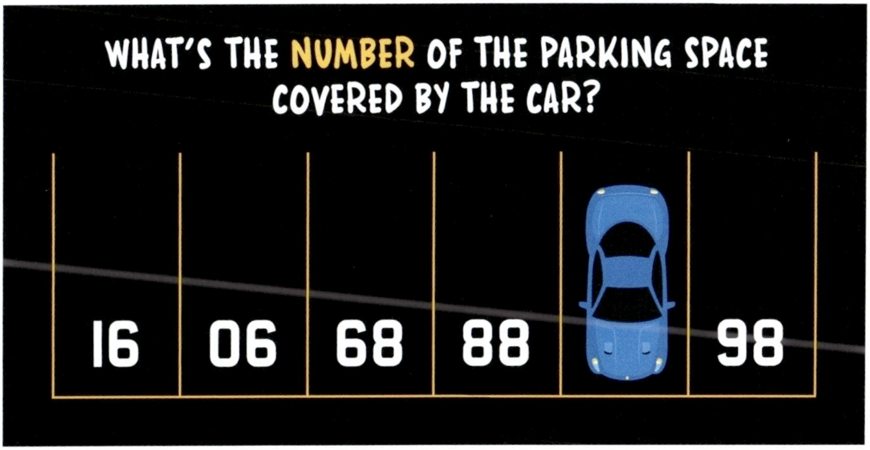

As you attempt to solve this puzzle, be conscious of your thought process. The real aim isn't the puzzle itself, but how you approach it.

Feeling stuck? Check the following page for a hint.

Solution-focused problem-solving is like finding the missing piece in a jigsaw puzzle: identifying the gap and filling it.

This kind of thinking is very appealing to our expertise — it's clear, it's efficient, and it's familiar. It's the mental equivalent of a well-trodden trail through the woods, leading reliably to a known destination.

HINT: TURN THE PUZZLE UPSIDE DOWN.

However, this preference can be a double-edged sword. The very knowledge that makes us valuable as an expert can also constrain us to the strategies we know best, potentially causing us to overlook more innovative solutions.

The solution to sticky problems, or the ones that don't have the kind of clear, linear jigsaw solution our expert brains prefer, is to **spend more time on the problem itself**: understanding it, dissecting it, zooming out, zooming in, and identifying the real goal of what we're trying to accomplish.

The worst thing we could do — the thing that wastes an outrageous amount of time — would be to come up with a good solution to the wrong problem.

So let's make sure we ask ourselves and our teams, "Is there a better problem to solve?" This question invites us to pause and reflect on whether the issue we're tackling is the right one, or if there's a more meaningful, impactful, or transformative problem to solve.

My favorite approach to finding the right problem is something I call the **Triple Zoom.**

First, Zoom In. Then, Zoom Out. Finally, Zoom Forward.

This is how you do it.

ZOOM IN

Ask, ***"What do I believe is the cause of the problem?"*** This is your chance to dive deeper into the problem to uncover its root causes, ensuring you're targeting the core issue.

ZOOM OUT

Ask, ***"Is there an even better problem to solve?"*** Here, you take a broader view to determine if there is a higher-level issue you could address.

ZOOM FORWARD

Ask, ***"How will this problem be different in a few years?***" How could we solve this issue for the changing environment rather than coming up with a solution today that immediately or eventually becomes obsolete?

What does the Triple Zoom look like in practice? Let me share an example.

For most of my life, I'd never given business advice with my pants down, but this particular Tuesday morning would change that.

I was at a dry needling appointment with my physical therapist and had to pull my pants down so she could dry needle my hips. (See my crazy tennis story in chapter 8 for a better explanation of the lengths I'm going to in pursuit of a big new goal.)

Anyhoo. I've got my pants down to my knees as my PT is sticking tiny needles into the sore muscles and then applying an electrical current to help them contract and release. As she's doing this, I ask her how business is going. (My favorite topic.) She says it's going really well, but she wants to find a social media manager. She asks if I have any recommendations about how to do that.

"OK!" I say. "I'm happy to help, but before I make any recommendations..." This is where I start my Triple Zoom.

ZOOM IN

"Why do you need a social media manager?" I ask.

She tells me that she wants to grow her business, but she already feels stretched thin running events, visiting doctors' offices to encourage referrals, conducting online webinars, writing a newsletter, sponsoring other people's events, and hosting online challenges. Not to mention, seeing patients.

This sounded to me like she'd fallen victim to the busyness trap, and I hypothesized that not all of her activities were yielding equal results.

ZOOM OUT

"Of all of those things that you are doing, what would you say are the top ways you bring new clients in the door?" I ask.

"Oh, no question!" she says. "It's personal referrals!"

Huh. That's interesting. That wasn't even on her list.

"And how do you get referrals?"

"Usually through something in our newsletter."

"Oh. Great. And how often do you send out your emails?"

"Not as often as we should. We're just too busy."

→→ ZOOM FORWARD →→

"Looking ahead, how do you want to be spending your time on your business in a few years?"

"I'd love to have more time to spend with patients and come up with a scalable way to grow that doesn't require as much time."

OK. So help me dissect this problem. Can you see that "finding a social media manager" might not be her real problem here? She's spending a lot of time and effort on many activities, but very little on the activity that drives the most business. What if instead of adding more to her plate, she hunted her zombie activities and freed up time and effort to increase referrals?

Bada bing, bada boom. We found a better problem worth solving. All with my pants around my knees. A real first for me.

The Triple Zoom is a helpful framework to tackle any challenge. But not all zooms are created equal. For me, the ROI on the middle zoom, Zooming Out, is greater than the others.

Trying to identify a better problem to solve can have a powerful impact on your organization.

Here's my favorite example of Zooming Out on a problem, from an organization near and dear to my heart: Veterans Community Project.

Veterans Community Project (VCP) is one of the most innovative nonprofits I have ever encountered. Their core mission is simple: End veteran homelessness one city at a time.

VCP builds villages of tiny houses that serve as a safe transition for homeless vets, and provides wrap-around services like dental assistance, transportation, mental health treatment, and even veterinary care for their pets. Basically, they offer whatever a veteran might need to get back on their feet.

When VCP's co-founders built their headquarters, they had to find a way to furnish the space, and they especially needed a big boardroom table for meetings with donors and staff. A typical nonprofit might ask, "How could we get this furniture donated?" Or "What's the cheapest furniture we could buy?" This conventional approach amounts to asking, "What's the least amount of money we can spend on this?"

The co-founders at VCP zoomed out and found a better problem to solve: "Could we actually make money with our furniture?" Rather than buy a boardroom table, they built one out of two-by-fours with a sheet of glass on top. Each two-by-four was sponsored by a supporting organization that wanted to be a long-term part of the VCP story. At $2,500 per plank, those organizations could add their logo and sign their names. Instead of costing thousands of dollars, VCP's boardroom table netted the organization $35,000 in donations.

Today, as VCP expands across the country, each new campus begins with a tradition: building a conference table and using it to raise local funding.

Spending more time on the problem and making sure we're asking the right questions encourages us to step outside the boundaries of conventional thinking and reframe the issue from a new angle. By shifting our perspective, we often reveal hidden solutions or unexplored opportunities within the problem itself.

This is the power of

SOLVING THE RIGHT PROBLEM.

Your challenge now is to bring this perspective to your everyday work. When faced with a problem, ask yourself not just how to solve it, but whether you're solving the right one.

A fresh perspective might just make all the difference.

How do we apply this to our work? With a little **Question Storming**.

This is an activity I love to do in my Curiosity workshops.

Once you come up with a problem you want to solve or a goal you'd like to achieve, instead of creating a to-do list of action items, start with a list of questions meant to help you better understand the problem.

First, ask yourself questions about the problem for four minutes. Nothing but questions. Help yourself understand the issue better.

Then, once you're done, it's still not time to jump to solutions. We need to dive even deeper into the problem.

Find one to three friends or colleagues who will spend four minutes asking you even more questions. Just share what you are working on and start the timer. They aren't allowed to offer any solutions, and you aren't allowed to answer their questions, because the point here is to see what kind of questions they ask.

What you'll find in this extremely powerful activity is that their questions will help you understand the problem better and they will shine a light on where you need to do more exploring. This is an important step before you generate solutions.

Reflection Questions:

1. *Can you think of a time when you jumped too quickly into solving the wrong problem?*

2. *What's a current problem you are trying to tackle that could benefit from more time spent understanding it?*

Habit 5

THE TOP 10 LIST

How to uncover your most innovative ideas

"If you want to have good ideas, you must have many ideas."

Linus Pauling

When we're problem solving, we rarely come up with more than one solution. It's like our expertise grabs onto the first idea and says, "I can make this work, let's go!"

Unfortunately, **our first idea is almost never our best idea**, and everyone in the room knows it. That's why they offer lackluster support like, "Sure, let's give it a try." Or "What could it hurt?"

You must resist moving forward with these initial ideas.

Think back to my plan to get a basketball scholarship to pay for college. I went after that idea because I saw a flyer. I wasted my entire sophomore year of high school — valuable time I could have used to work on approaches with better chances of success — banking on this flawed plan.

What if instead of going after my first idea, I sat down and made a list of 10 different ways I could get a scholarship to college, and then picked the most promising idea based on my skills and resources? How much do you want to bet that basketball wouldn't be at the top of that list?

This is the power of expanding our list of possible options, otherwise known as divergent thinking.

Your initial idea is likely to be the safest (my milk-only diet notwithstanding) — the low- hanging fruit of your expertise. But

SAFETY RARELY LEADS TO BREAKTHROUGHS.

By forcing yourself to come up with 10 ideas, you're stretching beyond the obvious and the easy.

The quote at the start of this chapter comes from Linus Pauling, the only person to win two Nobel Prizes in unrelated fields (one was the Nobel Prize for Chemistry; the other was the Nobel Peace Prize for his activism against nuclear weapons). His quote reflects a fundamental principle in innovative problem-solving: Not all ideas are born equal, and often, it's through the process of creating a multitude of options that the best one will surface.

It's a bit like panning for gold; you need to sift through a lot of sediment to find the real riches. The tool I use is the **TOP 10 LIST.**

And whenever I have a problem to solve, it's always one of my first activities, soon after I do something like the Triple Zoom (see previous chapter) to ensure I'm solving the right problem.

To create your Top 10 list, you simply write your problem at the top of a piece of paper and come up with 10 different solutions for how to address it.

Your first three ideas will probably come easily and be the most obvious. Around idea number

four, you'll feel the stretch. By seven, you'll start cursing my name and want to quit, but if you push through, you will tap into your subconscious mind and open sources of creativity and innovation that you never thought possible.

Here are some examples of how I've used Top 10 lists with clients:

- **Top 10 ways we could grow an important customer account**
- **Top 10 things we could do to increase the effectiveness of our digital marketing**
- **Top 10 places we could look to fill a really important role in our organization**
- **Top 10 articles we could write over the next few months to demonstrate thought leadership**
- **Top 10 ways we could improve the culture on our team**
- **Top 10 ways we could improve our customer experience**
- **Top 10 professional contacts we want to stay in touch with this year**
- **Top 10 things we want out of a new website**
- **Top 10 things we want to gain from our annual event**
- **Top 10 things we could do to make this list amount to 10 things**

Hopefully you get the idea! And the beauty here is that expanding beyond the first idea potentially gives us a bounty of good approaches: If three of the 10 ideas for improving team culture actually sound great, we can try them all. As experts, our strength lies not only in what we know but in our capacity to reach beyond it. Thinking beyond the obvious allows us to unlock more powerful, original, boundary-pushing approaches.

Give yourself the freedom to think broadly, think weirdly, think wrongly — because somewhere in that beautiful mess of thoughts, your best idea is waiting to be discovered.

Have you ever heard of the design thinking double diamond?

It's a visual representation of innovative problem solving that always reminds me about the need to spend the proper amount of time on both the problem and solution.

Imagine two diamonds side by side, each representing a phase of exploration and refinement. The first diamond focuses on identifying the right problem, and the second on identifying the right solution.

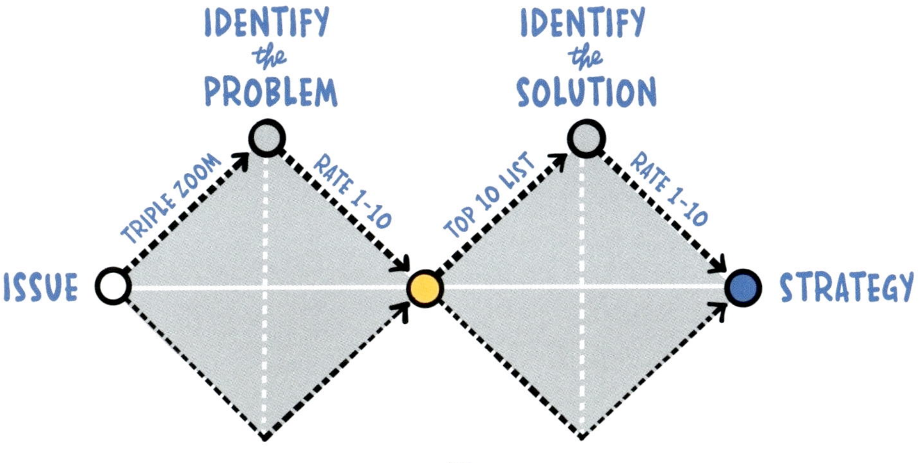

Here's how it works:

Identify the Problem (first diamond)

Step 1: **Diverge.** Spend more time on the problem to make sure you identify the best one. Use the Triple Zoom methodology to look at it from different angles.

Step 2: **Converge**. Once you identify a few options, focus on the problem that has the highest impact. Rate your options using the 1–10 Filter from Chapter 1 to find the gnarliest, juiciest problem to solve.

Identify the Solution (second diamond)

Step 1: **Diverge.** Use the Top 10 List to generate a wide range of potential solutions. Keep pushing until you reach those truly innovative ideas.

Step 2: **Converge**. Critically evaluate and prioritize your ideas. Use the 1-10 Filter to rate each one based on its potential impact and feasibility. This helps you narrow down to the most promising and effective solutions.

The beauty of the Double Diamond model lies in its structured yet flexible approach to problem-solving. It ensures that you don't rush to solutions without thoroughly understanding the problem first. And by dedicating time to both divergent and convergent thinking, you are less likely to miss out on innovative ideas and more likely to identify solutions that have a significant and lasting impact.

Ultimately, the Double Diamond model equips us with the tools and mindset needed to tackle complex problems with confidence and clarity. It reminds us that innovation is not a linear process but a dynamic journey that requires both exploration and refinement.

Plus, using the Double Diamond model gives you a great excuse for all those doodles during meetings:

Reflection Question:

What are some areas of your work that could benefit from a Top 10 list this week?

Habit 6

THE BETA TEST

How to use small bets to drive big innovations

"All life is an experiment. The more experiments you make, the better."

Ralph Waldo Emerson

When I was pregnant with our first child, my husband and I wanted to come up with a perfect name. After three months of deliberation, we were leaning toward naming our son True after the famous line from Hamlet:

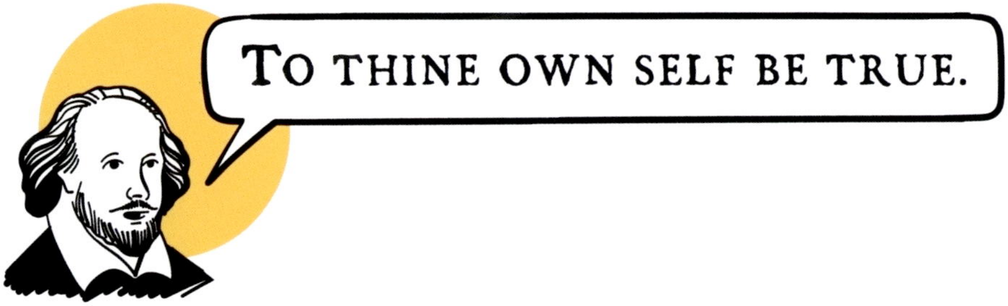

A close friend of ours, who also had a unique name (I'm doing him a solid by not using it here), begged us not to name our son True. Our friend was convinced we were about to ruin the boy's life. I was torn. I loved the name, but I wanted to respect our friend's opinion, and I didn't want to wait 20 years to find out whether we were wrong.

So I wondered, "How could I create a test to figure out which one of us is right?"

Here's the experiment I came up with: I found eight people on LinkedIn and Facebook named True – seven men and one woman ranging in age from 12 to 55 – and I contacted each one to ask for an interview.

In the interviews, I asked about what it was like to get teased as a child (I assumed everyone gets teased for something), go through school, apply for jobs, go to happy hours, and try to date. The conversations lasted about 30 minutes, and the stories I heard were surprisingly consistent. It turned out that people named True lived very similar lives!

They all got picked on in the same, mostly harmless way, they all had to come up with a way to clarify their name at happy hours because most people misheard it as "Drew," and they could all point to specific benefits in job hunting and dating directly attributable to being named True.

One man even emailed later to thank me for the conversation because he had never reflected on his life to such a degree.

My husband and I decided that was evidence enough, and at the time of this writing, my son True is 11 years old and pretty happy with his name. When he introduces himself to people, he says "True with a T" or "the opposite of False."

This experiment is a great example of a **BETA TEST.**

Every time we have a big new idea to bring into the world, the first thing we need to do is Beta Test it to decide whether it's a good use of our efforts. Think of this as a way to de-risk our investment.

The term "beta test" originates from the software development industry, where it refers to the first users to interact with a product. That's when all the big lessons are learned. As Mike Tyson famously said, "**Everyone has a plan until they get punched in the mouth**." And the Beta Test is our way of using a small investment of time and effort to uncover any hidden flaws or potential issues in our idea before stepping into the ring.

I believe so strongly in the Beta Test because my biggest professional failure came after I neglected to run one and instead let my "expertise" lead the way.

When I was 29, I had experienced a fair amount of professional success as an entrepreneur. I had a thriving services company (the one mentioned in chapter 3), was involved in several community groups, and really felt like I knew what I was doing. So I started dreaming even bigger.

I came up with an idea for a software product that would help refer attorneys to one another.

Every week attorneys get requests for legal help outside their area of expertise. And what they usually do is send an email to the lawyers they know asking who those people know that does this type of law. Like an estate lawyer trying to find an FDA attorney. And I thought, there's got to be a better way to do this manual process.

I raised nearly $500,000 in angel funding, hired a team, built the software, and convinced a regional bar association to promote it as an internal program. I called it Legal Sonar, and — like all startups in the 2010s — developed a cool logo and slapped it on a lot of t-shirts.

Legal Sonar sold a ton of memberships to lawyers. Signups were going so well that a venture fund called to ask what I'd do with an extra $1.5 million in funding.

But there was a problem.

Lawyers were signing up to be featured on the platform, but they weren't using it to actually find other lawyers to refer folks to. We tried everything we could imagine to change behavior, but nothing worked.

In a last-ditch effort, we ran a contest. We knew that lawyers were still sending these emails to their colleagues looking for referrals, so we said, don't even worry about the software, just CC help@legalsonar.com when you email your friends, and we'll email you ideas for lawyers who do this kind of work. And every time you CC that email you are entered to win a brand new iPad. And we're giving away one iPad a week. (This was 2010. iPads were really special then.)

So out of 10,000 members of the bar association who were told about this contest, how many do you think CCed the email address over the next month? Keep in mind: We emailed them about it, snail mailed them about it, and even called them to tell them about the contest.

How many did you guess?

The answer: zero.

Legal Sonar was a **ZOMBIE.**

I spent the next three months working hard to get our investors their money back (thankfully, we hadn't taken that $1.5 million) while simultaneously helping all eight of my employees find places to land. And I did this from what felt like the fetal position, because I was feeling sorry for myself.

After some time passed, I began to reflect on what had gone wrong. My ego, my desire to believe the Legal Sonar concept was good enough, had prevented me from properly testing or de-risking. Looking back, I didn't even need to build the software (spending hundreds of thousands of dollars) to learn whether the idea was a good one. I could have just run that email experiment that we ran at the end.

Think of what I could have accomplished with a complete do-over. That's what Beta Tests allow us to do.

I promised myself on that day that I would never again commit resources to an idea without having proof that it was going to work. And I vowed to help others avoid the same pain and loss by putting the lessons I learned into a book (more on that in a minute).

Did you know that Beta Tests are also a great way to win an argument with your boss?

When you have a disagreement with a supervisor about the best direction, they are always going to win, because they're the boss.

But instead of trying to debate them on who is right, what if you asked this:

Running a Beta Test is the source of one of my biggest wins as a consultant: helping a Fortune 500 company make an extra $8 million in revenue, in my first week there. Let me see if I can tell the story without giving away too many trade secrets.

The company is a financial services firm. One of its offerings is an online product that has a potential add-on at checkout. My first week at the company I met with the product owners who were trying to figure how to get more customers to choose the add-on.

"Why don't we just [do this very obvious idea]?" I asked.

"We've asked about [this very obvious idea] before, but the higher ups are worried about potentially upsetting customers. They've told us to never bring up [very obvious idea] again."

In most organizations this would be the end of the conversation. They've tried that before, it was a no-go, so let's move on to some more complicated solution.

But I just couldn't drop it. "What if we de-risked the idea with an experiment?" I asked.

"Like what?" the product owner asked.

"Well, what if we called some customers and told them that we're thinking about [very obvious idea] to gauge their reaction. Then if we don't hear any strong feelings from 20–40 phone calls, we could run another experiment by using [very obvious idea] for just 1% of the online customers to gauge their reactions. And if that is successful, then we could try it on 3%, then 5%, then 10%, with careful scrutiny for complaints at each step. What if we just took one tiny step at a time rather than arguing for the full change?"

They went for it. No one we called had strong feelings about the [very obvious idea]. As they began implementing the idea to the first 1%, no one complained. Neither did the next 5%, or the 10% after that.

The company successfully implemented [very obvious idea] with no complaints at all. And they made an extra $8 million that year as a result. Not too shabby.

That's the power of

EXPERIMENTATION.

It not only prevents you from investing in projects that have a low likelihood of success, it also helps you

REDUCE THE RISK OF INNOVATIVE IDEAS.

And it helps you get reluctant collaborators on board.

Your Beta Test can take place over a couple of hours or a few weeks, but the result is evidence you'll take with you as you pitch your boss. And evidence that your idea is sound is far more persuasive than a good idea alone.

Reflection Question:

What is an area of your work that could benefit from a Beta Test right now?

Habit 7

ITERATE TO GREAT

How to refine your way to a win

"Few ideas work on the first try. Iteration is key to innovation."

Sebastian Thrun

The Marshmallow Challenge is a fascinating design exercise that asks teams to build the tallest possible freestanding structure out of twenty sticks of spaghetti, one yard of rope, one yard of tape, and one marshmallow. You can do the challenge as a team-building activity, to learn about product design and creativity, or just for fun.

Teams get 18 minutes and the marshmallow has to go on top.

According to Tom Wujec, an author and multiple TED Talk speaker who helped popularize the exercise, all different kinds of groups take the Marshmallow Challenge: engineers, architects, business executives, recent graduates of business school, even kindergarteners. Consistently, the MBAs do worse than every other group of participants.

The average structure built is about 20 inches, but the MBAs are averaging just 10. Even kindergarteners are kicking their butts, building structures two and a half times taller.

How is this possible?

These are the very people that we're training how to plan and execute the ideas of the future. It all has to do with how they allocate their time.

The MBAs usually spend about the first 30% of the challenge planning the perfect structure and assigning roles. Then, 60% of their time building. And finally, with just a minute or so left, they place the marshmallow on top of the structure (very confidently), only to watch the entire thing collapse under the weight of that marshmallow.

The MBAs wait until the very end of the exercise, when they've already built the full structure, to interact with the most critical piece of the puzzle, that marshmallow. And they're so confident in their plan that they don't leave themselves any time to adjust. You know, just in case they're wrong.

The kindergarteners have a totally different approach. They start with a small and stable structure and put the marshmallow on top almost immediately. This takes just a few minutes, and now they have lots of time left to expand and experiment. They build something, see how it works, and try again. They don't believe there's one right answer to this puzzle.

THEY PLAY TO FIGURE IT OUT.

In the same time that the MBAs build just one structure, the kindergarteners are able to build four or five different versions. That's how they're consistently outperforming. Wujec has said they tend to build the tallest and most interesting structures.

To me, the lesson of this challenge is:

THE LONGER YOU WORK ON YOUR PLAN IN A VACUUM THE MORE LIKELY YOU ARE TO FAIL.

Even if your Beta Test is successful, don't spend all your resources on version one. Allocate your resources to give yourself five different iterations of an idea.

Otherwise, you're risking everything on plan A, and you know what they say about the best laid plans.

After Legal Sonar failed, I wanted to share the lessons I'd learned from the failure to save other entrepreneurs from feeling the same heartache, so I resolved to write a book detailing my lessons learned. But I wanted the book to be accessible to everyone rather than just experienced businesspeople, so I chose an unusual format: a novel.

Much like starting a business, writing a book is a bit of a gamble. The chances of getting an agent or signing a book deal with a major publisher are minuscule and writing an unconventional cross-genre book – like a business novel – is an even riskier bet. So – unlike with launching Legal Sonar – I didn't plan on version one being perfect. I planned to iterate my way to a final product.

I wrote a quick draft of the first half of the book and asked seven people in my target audience for feedback. I actually didn't tell them I was the one who had written it or what I was looking for in terms of feedback. I waited until they were finished and then asked them whether they found the story engaging and what key points they got out of it.

I made a list of six lessons I was hoping people would learn from the draft. And when the early readers told me their key takeaways, none of my six lessons made their lists. That was trouble.

Moreover, they told me they didn't care for the story or the characters, and that the main character (a man) sounded like he was written by a woman. Ouch.

So I went back to the drawing board and recalibrated.

I rewrote again and again, taking each new version back to test readers.

By the fourth draft, I had the general idea figured out but wanted to make faster revisions, so I started what I called a Reverse Book Club, assembling a group of friends every two weeks to help me read through new material and suggest changes.

Reverse Book Club members provided expert input on key topics of the book: cycling, poker, and entrepreneurship. And they helped make the writing and revising a lot more fun.

This process of iterating my way to success (seven considerably different drafts) helped me weave genuinely useful lessons into a truly compelling story. After its publication, All in Startup made its way to the *New York Times* and the *Wall Street Journal* bestseller lists. It's been published in several languages and used to teach entrepreneurship and innovation at more than 100 universities. And today, 10 years after publication, it is still selling significant numbers of copies each year, and I'm still receiving emails from entrepreneurs for whom it made a huge difference. Many of those emails validate the choice to weave the lessons into a business novel by telling me it's the only business book they've ever read cover to cover.

The book you're holding in your hand – just like all the others I've written – has gone through considerable rewrites. It's had fifty different title changes and at one point was structured around an acronym that drove my husband crazy because I was convinced I had to teach it out of order. He finally persuaded me by saying, "If it's out of order in the book, it's not an acronym!"

If you want a solution that stands the test of time and makes a considerable impact,

DON'T PLAN ON PERFECTION WITH VERSION ONE.

Give yourself the space to get there through a number of iterations, and be open to suggestions on where to make improvements.

Sometimes we inadvertently slow down work on our team by expecting version one to be perfect — or even by making our team think we expect perfection, whether we do or not. This causes panic, delay, and avoidance, and stifles creativity.

Believe it or not, even if you use the word "draft" when you ask for a document, the request can trigger a lot of fear. You might be unaware that a previous boss expected a polished final product with each draft and yelled at subordinates when it wasn't "right." You might be unaware of their self-created perfectionist tendencies.

So they stall and wait until the last second to bring you a document which is way off track. "How did we get here?" you wonder. "How could they possibly think this was the right direction? And they spent how much time creating this???"

You can use the idea of iteration to make a safe place for your colleagues to create a true draft.

I'll borrow a phrase from novelist and writing teacher Anne Lamott and call it the "Shitty First Draft (SFD)."

Shitty First Draft is such a beautiful term. It tells them exactly what you want. It helps you see how they are thinking about this project, and prevents them from spending too much time or energy in the wrong direction. It's like a pencil sketch of a painting. It's easy to make changes before the paint is on the canvas.

Asking for a SFD takes the pressure off and allows you to be true collaborators in the process. And they won't spend too much time just staring at their screen asking themselves, "Is this what she wants? Is this good enough?"

SFDs significantly increase the speed of work on your team and reduce time spent going in the wrong direction.

Additionally, when you want true feedback on a project, labeling the assignment a SFD will give others permission to be honest. By calling all initial drafts of my books SFDs, I elicit much more honest feedback from early readers.

Remember, the first version is never your best work. Give yourself the time and permission to make it as good as possible.

Reflection Questions:

1. Can you think of a time when you iterated your way to success? When the first version wasn't the right one?

2. What's something in your work that could benefit from a new version?

SECTION III
INCREASE YOUR LEARNING AGILITY

"The illiterate of the 21st century will not be those who cannot read and write, but those who cannot learn, unlearn, and relearn."

Alvin Toffler

The paradox of expertise is that as our knowledge in a particular area grows, our pace of learning diminishes.

To continue to excel, we must embrace a state of perpetual learning — a concept known as "learning agility." It's the ability to unlearn and relearn, to dismantle old frameworks and adapt to new information swiftly and adeptly.

It's not about mastering specific skills, but about developing the capacity to acquire new ones as needed. In Zen Buddhism, this idea of perpetual learning is called shoshin, or beginner's mind. Shoshin is a counterpoint to expertise, where — as we've discussed — we tend to become closed off to new ideas and stuck in our ways.

In a landscape that is continually reshaped by technology and globalization, the half-life of skills is shrinking. If we fail to adapt, what we know today may be obsolete tomorrow, and the success stories of today may become cautionary tales of complacency.

Learning agility, or shoshin, ensures that our expertise evolves, that it breathes and grows in step with the world around us.

This section is a call to arms for the established and the accomplished to not rest on their laurels but to lean into the discomfort of not knowing. It is an exploration of why the commitment to continuous learning is not only important but imperative for those who wish to continue to lead, to influence, and to make a mark on their fields.

Prepare to re-learn how to learn, with the speed and enthusiasm of those who know that their next discovery might just be their greatest.

Habit 8

NEVER GOAL ALONE

How to achieve any goal in record time

"None of us is as smart as all of us."

Ken Blanchard

About 10 years ago, I read a life-altering story.

The Great Ormond Street Hospital, a children's hospital in London, treats around 100,000 kids per year. In the '90s, Great Ormond Street was experiencing a horrific problem. Children were dying in between a successful surgery and moving to the intensive care unit. Something was wrong in the transition process, but the hospital just couldn't identify the cause. They tried everything they could, for almost 10 years!

The tricky part about "thinking outside the box" is realizing when you're stuck in one. And often, that box is created by years of this:

We as experts have the know-how for sure. But sometimes we need others to **challenge us** and **ask questions** that get the gears turning and the light bulbs popping.

One day, two of the Great Ormond Street surgeons were watching a Formula One race on TV and got an idea. What if they invited a Formula One pit crew to observe their transition process and provide feedback? Maybe those responsible for seamless, split-second tire changes and gas tank refills might have some ideas for improving the speed and precision of the hospital's patient moves.

Many at the hospital thought this was a silly idea, and — at first blush — you can see why. These two surgeons were imploring fellow esteemed medical professionals to ask car mechanics for advice. Their colleagues pushed back. The pit crew would need months of training just to understand what was happening in the surgery room; how could they possibly provide any value?

The two surgeons ignored the skeptics and forged ahead. Even though the Formula One pit crew didn't understand the medical procedures taking place, they quickly identified faults in the transition process:

- People were shouting over each other.
- People were plugging and unplugging things over one another.
- No single individual was in charge.
- No standard order existed for how the transition was to take place.
- The medical team didn't practice for the bad situations (the way a pit crew would practice for a car being on fire or operating in a storm).

Using the pit crew's fresh perspective, the surgical team addressed the blind spots they uncovered and transformed the hospital's procedures. This reduced errors by 66% and created a standard transition process that saved countless young lives.

The heroes of this story are the experts. They just needed a little help identifying the problem.

Thinking "outside the box" is necessary for innovation, but when we are in the box, our learning is limited, and innovation is nearly impossible. We need someone to pull us out — to give us **the perspective we cannot give ourselves.**

As experts, we tend to be action oriented and want to take the burden of an issue on our own shoulders. We ask ourselves, "How would I do this?" But the better question is often ***"Who can help me do this?"***

Turning to others for help isn't a sign of weakness or a waste of time. It will often help us get to a destination much faster than we could have on our own.

After learning about the Great Ormond Street Hospital story and the idea of pit crews, I became obsessed with the concept.

I thought to myself, would this work on me, at an individual level? Could I set a seemingly impossible goal and put together my own "pit crew" to help me accomplish it?

At the time, I just happened to have a goal that was going nowhere.

It was 2018 and I was working on my second book, *The Curiosity Muscle*. The book was a business parable in which one of the characters was attempting to do a 10-minute plank. And even though I personally couldn't muster more than a one-minute plank, I decided to try alongside the character in my book.

I mean, obviously I wasn't going to get to 10 minutes; that was impossible! But, I allowed myself to wonder, what if I could?

I did what anyone does when they set a goal: I tried my best. I went hard after the how. I went to the gym 5 days a week and tried to hold a plank as long as I could. "Volume!" I thought. "That ought to do it!"

Unfortunately, that didn't get me very far. After weeks and weeks of trying, I was up to two minutes but not budging past that.

My big goal felt out of reach.

That's when I learned the pit crew story and shifted my approach. This time, I focused on the who. I asked myself, "Who is really good at holding planks, and what do they know that I don't?"

I learned that the world record for holding a plank was over 10 hours. You read that right. So clearly, there was room for me to improve. And what the world record holders did was spend half their time strength training (aka lifting weights) on muscle groups that were apparently very important to holding a plank. I didn't know that several of these muscles even existed.

This was my first pit crew: I read every interview and every piece of content I could find about the record holders, and learned everything I could about their strategies.

I went back to the gym, started lifting weights to work these newly discovered muscle groups, and doubled my plank time in just a few weeks! I kept progressing. And every time I got stuck or plateaued in my achievement, I just went back and

FOUND A NEW WHO:

people who had systems to achieve big physical goals; people who specialized in mental practices that could help me hold a plank longer; people who knew how often I should practice to maximize my results.

I also wrote these same exercises into the planking character's journey in my book, which lent more credibility to the story.

After about six months of adding more and more "whos" to my pit crew, I held a plank for 11.5 minutes!

I know. Crazy!

As soon as I got up from that plank — and I mean the very second — I thought, "OK! Focusing on the *who* not the *how* really works. What's an even bigger challenge that I could try this way?"

That was 2018. Ever since, I've picked a **new stretch goal each and every year.**

It's still hard for me to believe that I achieved my first four seemingly impossible goals, all thanks to having the right whos in my corner. For handstands, I found a physical therapist who also taught handstands. He gave me all kinds of strength training ideas and practice exercises that I never would have thought of on my own.

For the pull-ups, I found a master's thesis written by Marine Major Misty Posey that argued women were fully capable of doing lots of pull-ups, but they were training all wrong. I reached out to Misty to understand her methodology and turned her into the founding member of my pull-up pit crew. I also shared a post on Instagram saying that I wanted to start a group for women trying to do their first pull-up. 35 women joined my group and shared encouragement and feedback on what was working and what wasn't.

The splits goal was actually more time intensive than challenging. It turns out there are a lot of people trying to do the splits and lots of pit crew members out there to show you exactly how to train and master it. I went through three different coaches before I found one whose methodology worked for me. Then it was just 30 minutes a day of swinging my leg side to side. To make it more fun, I found another mom

who was interested in learning the splits and added her to my pit crew to share daily progress and encouragement.

My biggest takeaway from first struggling with the plank to then having success in four separate goals is that

OUR EXPERTISE CAN SABOTAGE OUR GROWTH.

It lulls us into thinking that because we are successful in one part of our lives, we can just figure out how to do anything.

And when the new thing we try doesn't match that level of expected success relatively quickly, our expert thinking will step in and say, "this just isn't possible for me." And we will come up with some smart sounding excuses for why it will never happen. Excuses like, "I'm just too old." Or "My body isn't built for this." Or "I have tiny hands."

Innovative thinking says, **"If this is possible, then it's only a matter of time, and the right pit crew will get me there."**

And I'm going to keep testing this theory to see just how far I can push it. At the time of this writing, I have set the most ambitious personal challenge I've ever dared.

Last year I learned about the Maccabiah Games, or the "Jewish Olympics." It is the third largest sporting event in the world, after the World Cup and the actual Olympics. 10,000 athletes go to Israel every four years to compete in Olympic events. And the best part is that there are age brackets!

Ever since I learned about this event, I wanted to go. This would be my first ever time playing sports competitively! And even though I had just started playing tennis, I chose it as my sport.

2024 stretch goal: Make it to the Maccabiah Games (by qualifying for team USA) in tennis.

This challenge will mean going from a tennis novice who literally just learned the rules to a collegiate level player in just under two years.

This is my fifth stretch goal, so I've really stepped up my pit crew game. I just keep repeating to myself, "Never Goal Alone!" And the bigger the challenge, the more people I need on my team.

Here's my current pit crew:

- A tennis coach to help me make sure I'm developing all the right skills
- A trainer (my husband) to help me recover well after playing and hold me accountable to my strength training regimen
- A physical therapist to help me strengthen the right muscles and make adjustments when something starts to hurt
- A pelvic floor physical therapist to make sure that all of my body can keep up with this level of play, and dry needle muscles that need it
- A sports nutritionist to help me fuel my body correctly to keep up with a very high level of training

All of these individuals are helping me improve in ways I could never figure out on my own.

If you want to achieve something new or start growing at an exponential rate, the key is to **assemble a pit crew** with the knowledge to uncover your blind spots and help you think outside the box. And as you can see from my examples, this can be as simple as learning from online courses and interviews, or as complex as putting together a group of professionals. It's up to you. My rule of thumb is every time you hit a plateau, just level up your WHO.

And yes, my tennis goal sounds like a part-time job. But just like my full-time job, I'm loving every second. And I'm actually making progress!

If you want to follow along with my journey to the Maccabiah Games, just follow me on LinkedIn or Instagram.

And if you have your own stretch goal and want me to be a part of your pit crew and offer a fresh perspective, just reach out!

Reflection Questions:

1. Could any of your current projects or challenges benefit from a pit crew?

2. Who would you invite to be on that pit crew?

Habit 9

LEARN FROM THE WINS

How to increase your rate of improvement

"A good outcome doesn't mean you made a good decision."

Annie Duke

Did you know that it's actually ***difficult to learn from our successes?***

We usually assume that since things worked out, we did everything correctly. But in reality,

NOTHING IS EVER 100% A SUCCESS OR 100% A FAILURE.

And when we ask, "Was it successful?" we miss a huge opportunity to learn and improve.

Researchers refer to this as **outcome bias**.

In a 2015 study, BYU professors examined how outcome bias affected the strategic choices made by professional basketball coaches following close games. Specifically, they compared adjustments made in the wake of a close loss to those made after a close win.

In basketball, both a close win or a close loss means that a team played fairly equally to their opponents. Despite this, the researchers found that the coaches were much more likely to change their strategy after a close loss than after a close win.

This is a major missed opportunity. Let's not waste the chance to learn and adjust from our wins. Let's stop asking "Was it successful?" and ask a more important question.

I like to use a tool called the

AFTER ACTION REVIEW

to answer this question. After Action Reviews acknowledge that no matter how well things are going, there are always opportunities to improve, and we're going to work as a team to consistently uncover those opportunities and get better with every project.

At a very basic level, an AAR involves discussing how it went, what we learned, and what can be improved and how; all in a setting and tone that promotes psychological safety, honesty, and self-awareness.

The key is making space for the conversation.

If it's a short project, like an event, you can schedule an AAR right after the project is over. Or for a long-term project, you could consider doing an AAR after the first quarter, or at a regular cadence such as every couple of weeks.

This is the conversation that will help you iterate your way to success.

Let me make a strong suggestion that you schedule out your AARs at the beginning of the project to make sure they are on the calendar.

The other key is that you can't schedule AARs only when something goes wrong. Your team will assume that you're just looking for someone to blame. According to Annie Duke (quoted on page 123), if you want your collaborators to be forthcoming during an AAR of a project that didn't go smoothly, you must schedule them as part of regular business, which means holding them after successes too.

AARS HAVE TO BE A PART OF THE CULTURE.

Duke's rule of thumb is that you need six AARs on projects that go well for every one AAR on a project that goes poorly.

I use this tool after every keynote. And no matter how many times I've done it, I just go slide by slide within an hour of giving a speech and I always come away with a long list of tweaks I'd like to make — and sometimes a big idea for a future version. You'll have a long list too if you just give yourself the space to reflect!

We can improve so much faster by making constant small tweaks versus waiting for one big reset when things go poorly.

To download my After Action Review facilitation guide, visit www.DianaKander.com/Better.

Reflection Questions:

1. What is a recent win that you think has a hidden treasure trove of learning opportunities for improvement?

2. What's an area of your work that could benefit from regular AARs?

Habit 10

FAIL FORWARD

How to use setbacks as stepping stones to success

"Success is stumbling from failure to failure with no loss of enthusiasm."

Winston Churchill

When something doesn't work out, and our expertise is threatened, we become so eager to move on that we typically throw out everything associated with the project.

Many organizations I've worked with have all these interesting ideas that didn't work out, and no one knows about them because the organization regards them as embarrassing.

But as previously mentioned, rarely is anything ever 100% a failure or a success. Some good came out of that failed attempt, and very likely — in addition to the lessons learned — there are assets left over that we can reinvest in the future.

Those assets might be relationships, insights, intellectual property, tools, or systems and processes developed along the way.

Without taking the time to stop and reconsider them, these assets get lost forever.

Some people are defined by their failures, while others seem to grow even stronger and more powerful as a result. This ability to

FIND ASSETS AMONG THE RUBBLE

makes all the difference.

The concept of learning agility isn't just about acquiring new knowledge; it's also about the ability to unlearn outdated information and relearn in the face of new challenges. This adaptability is crucial when dealing with setbacks. By viewing failures as opportunities to uncover valuable assets, you continuously evolve and improve, making yourself truly failure proof.

Every setback is a chance to iterate and refine. Just as we embrace a beginner's mind to stay open to new ideas, we also must develop the mindset to see beyond the immediate disappointment of failure and identify the useful elements in every setback that could be repurposed for a future use.

You know, I haven't published every book I've ever written.

Sometimes I'll go through the process of writing 60,000, 80,000 or even 120,000 words of a book, just to realize that it's not good enough or that I don't really like teaching the subject matter.

Remember the 1–10 scale that helps you filter for a Yes? Well, these book projects are 4s, 5s, and 6s — maybe they started out as great ideas, but they somehow turned into zombies.

But I don't just throw the drafts away, because they contain elements that could be 9s and 10s.

I keep a whole repository of projects that never took off. And every now and then, I look at this repository for inspiration. I've got books, training programs, journal ideas, master classes, and many more concepts in a folder labeled, "Not Ready Yet," and those assets get incorporated into subsequent projects, improving every new thing I create.

In fact, this chapter on pulling great assets from your failures is a core idea from an entire book I wrote, but decided not to publish, about failure.

This isn't about looking at the bright side of a bad situation. It's about looking for the great stuff left behind after something doesn't work out.

My favorite example of this principle is the Amazon Fire Phone.

Some call it Amazon's biggest failure. Six months after launching a phone that was to replace all phones, they shut down the program and wrote off a $170 million loss.

What an embarrassment, right?

I interviewed the product manager for the Fire Phone. And wouldn't you know it, he didn't even see it as a big failure because of all the assets that the project created.

Even though customers didn't really care for the phone as a whole, they did like the voice assistant feature. So Amazon took the engineers working on the project and moved them to work full time on developing this feature and putting it into other hardware

products. They called her Alexa, and today she is in watches, TVs, cars, computers, and even refrigerators.

And Alexa wasn't even the biggest asset they found.

The product owner told me that in order to create your own phone (free of licensing fees to Google and with your own branding), you have to create your own maps app. And to do that, Amazon hired hundreds of people to build out navigation capability to map out every part of the world. That infrastructure also moved after the phone project was shut down and became the backbone of the Amazon delivery platform. Think about it: You didn't see any Amazon trucks on the road until after the Fire phone flopped.

How much money do you think they are saving each year by having their own delivery platform? How much innovation are they opening for the organization by investing in this key part of their

operations? The $170 million loss pales in comparison to the growth created as a result. If you think about it, it's not really a loss at all, because they turned the project into a highly lucrative investment.

And all from finding those assets.

Learning agility requires us to shift our perspective on failure. Instead of seeing it as an end point, we see it as a step in our ongoing journey of growth. When Amazon's Fire Phone didn't succeed, they didn't just move on — they dug into the project's remnants and found gold.

Being successful isn't about never failing — it's about constantly evolving, learning, and finding value even in the setbacks.

Remember, if at first you don't succeed, skydiving probably isn't for you — but for everything else, just yell, "Plot twist!" and keep experimenting, keep iterating, and keep moving forward. Each failure is a forward step leading you to your next breakthrough.

Embrace the process, laugh at the missteps, and know that your greatest accomplishments are often hidden in the most unexpected places.

Reflection Questions:

1. What is a past failure that you think still has some valuable assets?

2. What are the potential assets from that project?

YOUR BEST TEACHER
is
YOUR LAST MISTAKE

CONCLUSION

How to get really good at getting better

"We keep moving forward, opening new doors, and doing new things, because we're curious and curiosity keeps leading us down new paths."

Walt Disney

When I was in my early twenties, I became obsessed with the idea of peaking. From where I started in the Soviet Union, it felt like every level reached was as good as it was going to get.

I distinctly remember having the kind of money that allowed me to order soda at restaurants (an impossible extravagance during my childhood) or to be able to shop at Target. You know, huge life accomplishments.

It was getting harder and harder to imagine that life could get any better.

I would constantly ask my husband, "Is this it? Is this the year we peak? Is it all downhill from here?"

I would make my passwords include the year I thought was going to be my peak year. (Please don't try to hack my accounts!)

I didn't realize it at the time, but the status quo gravitational pull was slowing me down. It was getting harder and harder to imagine a better future, and therefore harder to take action to make it happen.

And then a funny thing happened. I started implementing the innovation habits we've just worked through, and I found that ***there's always another level to unlock***. There is no finish line to getting better.

THE ONLY LIMITATION TO YOUR FUTURE GROWTH IS YOUR OWN IMAGINATION.

This year my husband and I cofounded a brand-new sports and media company, helped raise a record amount of donations for the charities we care about, and were featured on 60 Minutes for rescuing and adopting three Afghan families. And it feels like we're just getting warmed up.

Believing that we can be better isn't about ignoring what we've already done. It's about building on our expertise and remaining open to new ideas and methods. It's about asking big questions and not getting stuck in old habits.

And when we refuse to settle for what we've accomplished and see ourselves as innovators, we will continue to find big opportunities for growth.

This book isn't asking you to take a giant leap into something new and different. Instead, think of it as a step back to a place you've been before. Remember the wonder and curiosity you had on day one of the job you're in right now? The fresh perspective you brought, untainted by routine and familiarity? We are all innovators on Day One.

Now, imagine if you could bottle up that first-day buzz and take a swig every morning? Think about it. What epic feats could you pull off? How might your view of "impossible" change?

The best experts are always learning. Isn't it reassuring to hear your doctor say, "You know, I just read an article about a new technology." Or, "There was a trial recently that totally proved this wrong."

Innovators know that there's always something new out there, a fresh angle or a groundbreaking approach. And that's exciting! It means there's always room to grow, to improve, and to make a bigger impact.

Your expertise is your **LAUNCHPAD**, not your landing zone. Your superpower is not just your ability to rack up skills but to **REMIX THEM,**

FLIP THEM, and

EXTEND THEM

in uncharted directions.

So, start each day as if it were Day One. Make time in your calendar for big questions like, "What are ten things we could try?" or "Who could give us a fresh perspective on this?" and "Where are we missing the breakthrough opportunity?"

And don't just desire to be more innovative. Make space for it within your schedule. Set time aside for After Action Review reflections (Habit 9), zombie-hunting discussions (Habit 2), and reimagine meetings (Habit 3). Don't just rush to solutions – use the double diamond (Habit 5) to stay in the problem for a bit longer.

Even 30 minutes per week dedicated to these activities can make a huge impact.

The formula is simple: If you want to make sure that your best days are ahead of you, then approach each day with the fresh eyes of a rookie and the wisdom of a sage. Stay curious and never stop reimagining what is possible.

To download my Day One Reset (a helpful tool to reconnect with your Day One self), visit www.DianaKander.com/Better.

And check out the back of this book! It's designed to sit on your desk and remind you each morning that it's always Day One.

Reflection Questions:

1. How could you make space for curiosity in your life?

2. Who would you need to involve in this new goal to ensure that it's a success?

EPILOGUE:

My Day One poem

I often conclude my keynotes with a poem about how I stay in the Day One mindset. Many have asked me to share that concluding poem, so here it is:

My strongest memory as a child is at the age of eight,
The night my family escaped the Soviet Union, seeking a better fate.

I remember hiding in my aunt's apartment after plan A had gone astray,
My parents looked frazzled and scared and I was just hoping they would find some way.
At midnight, we loaded on a bus, guarded by armed escorts, their faces stoic.
Leaving behind everything we knew; it felt the opposite of heroic.

It was me, my mom, my dad, and my grandma, rushing to catch a train,
Only one suitcase per person. Not much left of the life we used to lead, but enough to escape the pain.
And we knew so little about what was in store,
That one of those four suitcases was almost half full of just toilet paper galore!

A six-month journey led us to freedom here in the land of opportunity,
We arrived with no English, no money, and zero community.

So how did I get from that 8-year-old girl to the woman that was chosen to stand before you today?
My secret is simple, that little girl just never went away.

My inner 8-year-old, she embodies the essence of Snoop Dogg, an ever-evolving beat,
And refuses to let me become a Vanilla Ice, and get stuck on repeat.
She learned her lessons from the failed milk-drinking quest.
And now uses it as a reminder that not every idea is worth giving our best.

She whispers: Let's use 1–10 to raise the bar,
And never get stuck on a mountain of shoulds and coulds that rank subpar.
Let's slay the zombies, she says, that sap and drain,
And make sure that only the worthy projects remain.

Inside each of us, that curious 8-year-old resides,
Offering to help, with wonder that never subsides.
What do they know about our industry? How can they even participate?
They are experts at nothing; that is their strongest trait.

However you grew up…whatever your career has done,
Each morning is an opportunity to embrace that inner 8-year-old and make today Day One.
Unleash that innovator within and let them ask away,
You will change the lives of others, make a difference — please, she and I invite you…start today.

ACKNOWLEDGMENTS

Every morning I wake up to a very specific gratitude practice. I learned about it in a TedX ("Happy Brain: How to Overcome Our Neural Predispositions to Suffering," by Amit Sood, MD). It's a science-backed way to increase your happiness and life satisfaction. I've linked it for you below.

Silently and to myself, I thank three or four people in my life for something very specific, then I thank someone who is deceased, and then I thank a younger version of myself for some decision I made.

I thought I would start this acknowledgement section in a similar way.

I'd like to thank the following people for their impact on me:

My husband Jason. We've been together since we were 17 years old. That's a long time. We've become very different versions of ourselves at various times in our lives. And yet through it all, what's never changed is our belief in one another, our support of one another, and our ideal of trying to change the world for the better. Thank you for being my number one fan, my editor, my best friend, and the person who welcomes each crazy idea with a smile and an attitude of adventure.

My parents. Thank you for the example that you set. I often ask myself if I could make the decision at the age of 30 to leave everything I knew behind, not knowing where I was going or how I would survive. What an incredibly brave decision you made for our family. Thank you for the work ethic you demonstrated and the entrepreneurial spirit you instilled in me from a young age. Thank you for helping to take care of my little ones to allow me to travel the world to share my message. And thank you for coming over to our house to fix all the stuff we don't know how to fix.

Maddy Fredrick, my Chief of Staff. Thank you for the care and attention you show to our family and for being a utility player on the team. You are my right hand, my strategic thought partner, my source of honest feedback, my accountability coach, and my friend. I feel so grateful to get to work with you every day.

Karen Harris, Rebecca Clark, and the **CMI team.** Karen and Rebecca manage my keynote speaking business. But more than that, they are my thought partners and my gentle nudgers to never settle and keep innovating. Thank you for the amount of time you invest in our relationship, above and beyond what it would take to run the business well. Thank you for the singing telegram when

I had cancer (that was hilarious). Thank you for the handmade postcards. Thank you for taking a chance on me when I had very little, and for helping me prioritize my family when we had a lot. I couldn't imagine a better group of people to work with. (I'm currently crying as I write this.) Thank you to Karen and Rebecca and Carolyn and Maya and Madi and Dani and Sam and Julie and Palmira and the many other talents that make CMI what it is.

Sarah Whitten. Sarah was my first manager. She took me on after I gave one paid speech. And I went from her smallest management client to her biggest. We tragically lost Sarah in December of 2021, but her spirit has not left me. Thank you for everything you taught me. Thank you for your infectious energy. Thank you for your unwavering support. I still read a text or email of yours at least once per week. I think I fell in love with this business because I got to do it with you from the very beginning.

And these are the people who helped bring this book to life:

Drew Dernavich is the cartoonist that made this book so fun and accessible. I'm sure this project was a lot more than you bargained for, but I can't thank you enough for turning my message into a work of art.

My editor **Anna Maltby Patil.** Thank you for the time and attention you put into this book, including the research, which really felt above and beyond. I can't wait to work with you again.

My friend **Jun Han Chin** who contributed two amazing images to this book: the puzzle graphic on page 24 and the basketball image on page 127. I love watching you explain complex ideas in simple pictures.

My team of early draft readers who provided feedback and ideas for the book: **Jason Kander, Maddy Fredrick, Sam Demma, Ashley Good, Joshua Berry, Erin Slattery** and **Jessie Jacob**. These folks also happen to be some of my favorite people to spend time with.

And thanks to **you** for making it all the way to the end. They say we have decreased attention spans, but look at you, you're hanging in there. I feel like there should be a prize or something for getting to the end.

Why don't you send me a text and tell me what you thought? (816) 399-0084.

Diana

OTHER BOOKS BY DIANA KANDER

"Kander and Trotter will rescue your pitch from mediocrity and transform it into something unforgettable and undeniable. Packed with great stories and savvy tips, this book will help everyone become a smarter seller."

DAN PINK, #1 *New York Times* bestselling author of *The Power of Regret, Drive*, and To *Sell Is Human*

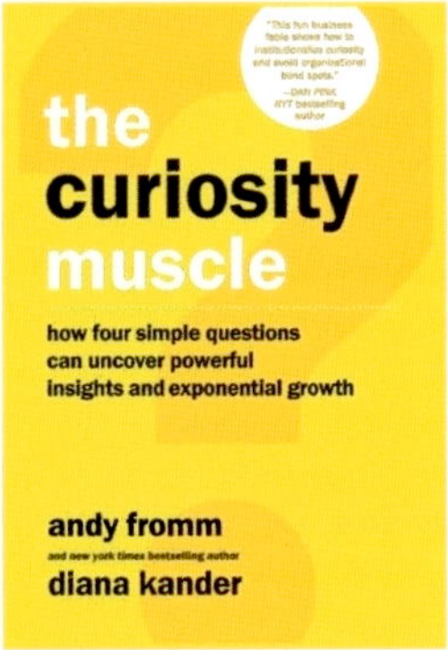

"*Curiosity* is the elixir for an engaged life and the foundation for a creative and innovative company. This beautifully written parable reminded me why thinking like a four-year old can be healthy for both employees and an organization."

CHIP CONLEY, *New York Times* bestselling author

"I dare you to find a business book for innovators that's as useful as *All In Startup*, and I double-dare you to find one that's as much fun to read. Diana Kander captures what it's like to launch something new. The result is a book that helps set readers on the path to finding innovation success."

TONY HSIEH, CEO of Zappos.com and author of the #1 *New York Times* Bestseller *Delivering Happiness*

ABOUT THE AUTHOR

When Diana Kander was just 8 years old, she and her family escaped the Soviet Union, entered the United States as refugees, and resettled in Kansas City without money or the ability to speak English.

And yet it is from these humble beginnings that Diana has achieved much success:

- As a Georgetown-educated attorney
- A university professor
- A founder of 10 companies
- A consultant to Fortune 500 companies and government leadership teams
- A *New York Times* bestselling author whose books have been taught in more than 100 universities and translated into many languages.

And her parents would like you to know that her sister is a doctor.

Diana has truly cracked the code on how curiosity can serve as the catalyst for exponential growth, and she thrives on helping individuals understand that they can get better results if they learn how to ask better questions.

Also, she can juggle. And do a handstand. Though not both at the same time…yet.

ABOUT THE ILLUSTRATOR

I'm Drew Dernavich.

I not only drew all of the illustrations in this book, but I did the entire design and layout as well. Which was a first for me!

But this wasn't just a job. It was a collaboration. Diana said "hey, let's do something cool!" How could I say no? I wish every project started off that way.

And readers, you should know that Diana walks the talk where innovation is concerned. She experiments, she is enthusiastic about new directions, she loves the push and pull of debating ideas, is a good listener, and is a good decision maker. This book was a joy to create.

When I'm not doing it in book form, you can find me taking large-scale graphic notes at meetings and conferences, often with real pens and markers.

I also am a regular cartoonist for *The New Yorker* magazine, where you may recognize me by my "woodcut" style. I've written two children's books and am working on another.

And, fun fact: I have a license to drive a forklift, although I haven't had the opportunity to do that in a while, which is probably a good thing.

AND NOW...

GET CURIOUS!